SCIENCE WIDE OPEN

# Women in Engineering

Written by Mary Wissinger
Illustrated by Danielle Pioli

Science, Naturally!
An imprint of Platypus Media, LLC
Washington, D.C.

Who builds bridges?

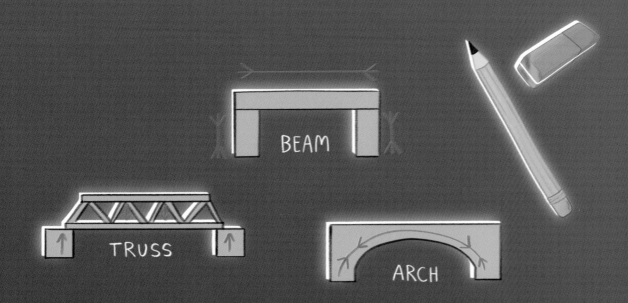

Building a bridge is a balancing act. It takes many people, lots of equipment, and a talented engineer to put it all together.

Brooklyn Bridge
completed in 1883

Emily Warren Roebling didn't set out to be an engineer.
She lived in a time when women were discouraged
from doing things like expressing opinions and having
careers. Emily did both when she helped build the
Brooklyn Bridge. It wasn't easy. The suspension bridge
was over a mile long, making it the longest suspension
bridge in the world at the time.

Emily Warren Roebling
(EM-i-lee war-en ROH-bling)
United States, 1843–1903

Civil Engineering

Emily took on the role of chief engineer in place of her husband, who had become too sick to do the job. She oversaw bridge construction for more than ten years, from managing workers to coordinating supplies.

She wore a skirt and petticoat because women of the time weren't allowed to wear pants. Construction can be dangerous work, especially without the right clothes, but that didn't stop her from visiting the site.

When Emily and her team of workers finally finished
the bridge, she rode across it in a carriage. She carried
a rooster—a symbol of victory at the time—to celebrate
her success. Emily's engineering work still matters
today. Hundreds of thousands of people cross the
Brooklyn Bridge every week.

# What is engineering?

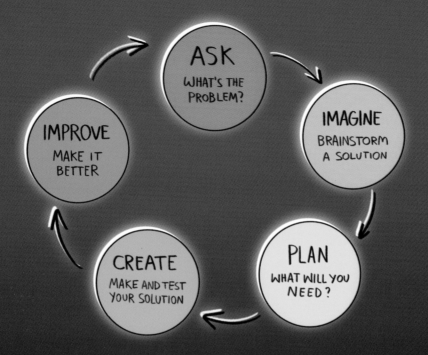

At its heart, engineering is solving problems.

To do this, engineers use science, math, design, creative thinking, and persistence. Engineers do many different types of work, from building bridges to solving health problems. They also create and improve things that we use every single day.

Things we use every day?
Like what?

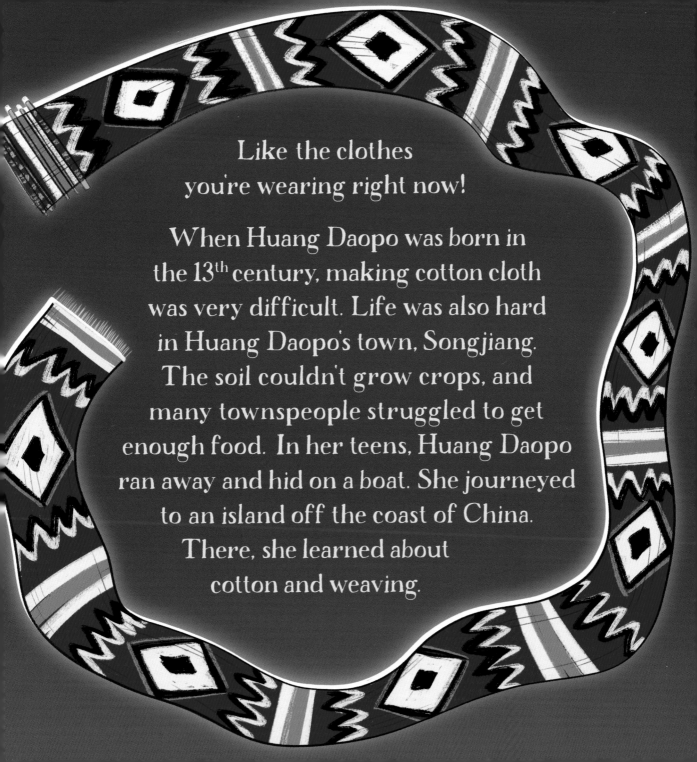

Like the clothes
you're wearing right now!

When Huang Daopo was born in
the 13th century, making cotton cloth
was very difficult. Life was also hard
in Huang Daopo's town, Songjiang.
The soil couldn't grow crops, and
many townspeople struggled to get
enough food. In her teens, Huang Daopo
ran away and hid on a boat. She journeyed
to an island off the coast of China.
There, she learned about
cotton and weaving.

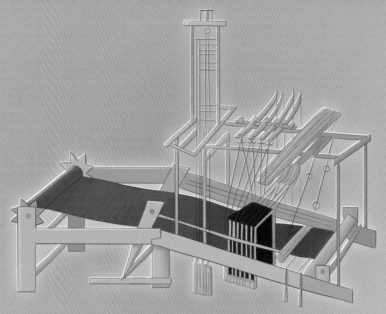
Fabric Weaving Loom

When Huang Daopo returned to Songjiang as an adult, she used her knowledge to help the town. She created a machine to clean raw cotton quickly and built a spinning wheel that could spin many threads at once. She invented these revolutionary machines 500 years before anyone else figured out how to make them.

Her town became known for weaving beautiful cotton fabrics, quilts, and mattresses. Huang Daopo's inventions brought jobs and security to many people.

# Mechanical Engineering

Huang Daopo
(*huahng dow-poh*)
China, 1245–1330

So engineers are inventors?

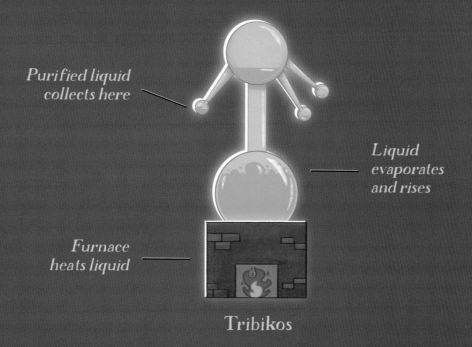

Purified liquid
collects here

Liquid
evaporates
and rises

Furnace
heats liquid

Tribikos

Engineers have been inventing for thousands of years.

Mary the Prophetess lived in Egypt nearly 2,000 years ago, and she loved experimenting with metals, liquids, and laboratory equipment. But the tools of the time were not advanced enough for her big ideas, so Mary invented her own—like the tribikos. Her inventions were important for alchemy, an early study of the natural world that led to modern chemistry.

Mary's most famous invention is still used today: the heated water bath. This technology allows scientists to run experiments, helps factories produce food, and is also used in wastewater plants.

People even use heated water baths at home to soften wax for candles, melt chocolate for desserts, and slowly cook things like tasty cheesecakes. This invention is still called the *bain-marie*, meaning "Mary's bath."

Mary the Prophetess
(MARE-ee the PRAH-fet-ess)
Egypt, First Century CE

Chemical Engineering

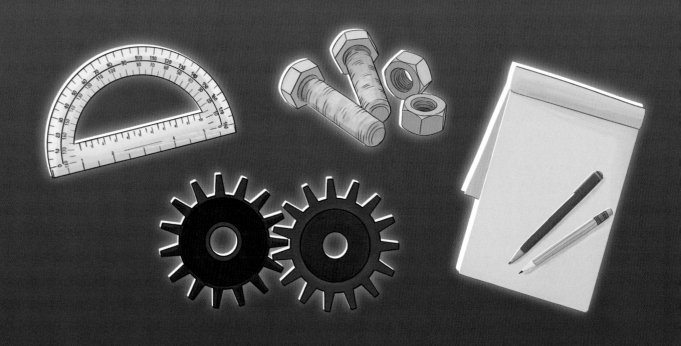

What else do engineers do?

Engineers think creatively.

When movie star Hedy Lamarr wasn't making films, she worked on projects in her laboratory. She had lots of ideas for inventions and experiments, such as making tablets that turned water into soda. Hedy also created designs for a more aerodynamic airplane, based on the smooth shape of fast birds and fish. She even kept a small laboratory in her on-set trailer so she could work between scenes.

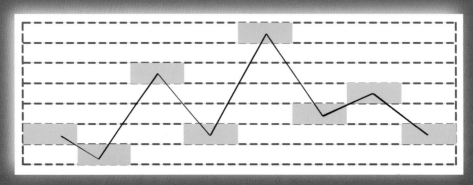

Frequency Hopping

Then Hedy learned that important radio messages sent during World War II were being blocked. It wasn't long before she came up with an idea for a secret communication device. Her device could send the radio messages hopping around to different frequencies, making them impossible to find and jam.

She and a friend developed and patented the device, but most people laughed it off. Still determined to help, Hedy used her fame to raise millions of dollars for the war effort.

RADIO
TECHNOLOGY

ENT
AW

**Electrical Engineering**

Hedy Lamarr
(HED-ee la-MAR)
Austria & United States, 1914–2000

Later, her idea of frequency hopping was used when creating technologies like cell phones, Wi-Fi, Bluetooth, GPS, and even military communications. Hedy's work is especially important since we use these technologies in our daily lives and to help us solve problems.

$$f(x + iy) = \sum_{k=1}^{\infty} \frac{1}{k^{(x+iy)}}$$

$$S = \sum_{k=1}^{n} f\left(a + k\frac{b-a}{n}\right)\left(\frac{b-a}{n}\right)$$

$$14\sqrt{x} + 15 = 71$$

# What other kinds of problems can engineering solve?

Problems like climate change.

Sandra Cauffman has worked at NASA for many years, helping to design, build, and launch equipment to study Earth, our Sun, the solar system, and the universe. The information she gathers helps us discover how the universe works and even find other planets similar to Earth. Many of her projects also help us understand our planet and its changing climate, so we can develop technologies to solve problems facing our future.

GOES-16
Geostationary Operational
Environmental Satellite

If you've checked the weather lately, the forecast
probably came from a satellite that Sandra helped
develop. Satellites monitor Earth and send back
information about the temperatures, ice caps, coral
reefs, and even mosquitos. That data can be used for
forecasts and emergency alerts, saving many lives.

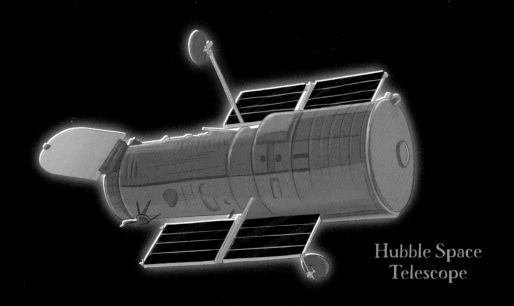

Hubble Space
Telescope

Sandra also worked on the Hubble Space Telescope
First Servicing Mission and helped lead a team that
sent a spacecraft to study the atmosphere of Mars.
Missions to space are complicated and take years of
preparation. Sandra coordinates the many engineers,
scientists, and specialists who work together to give
us a glimpse into outer space.

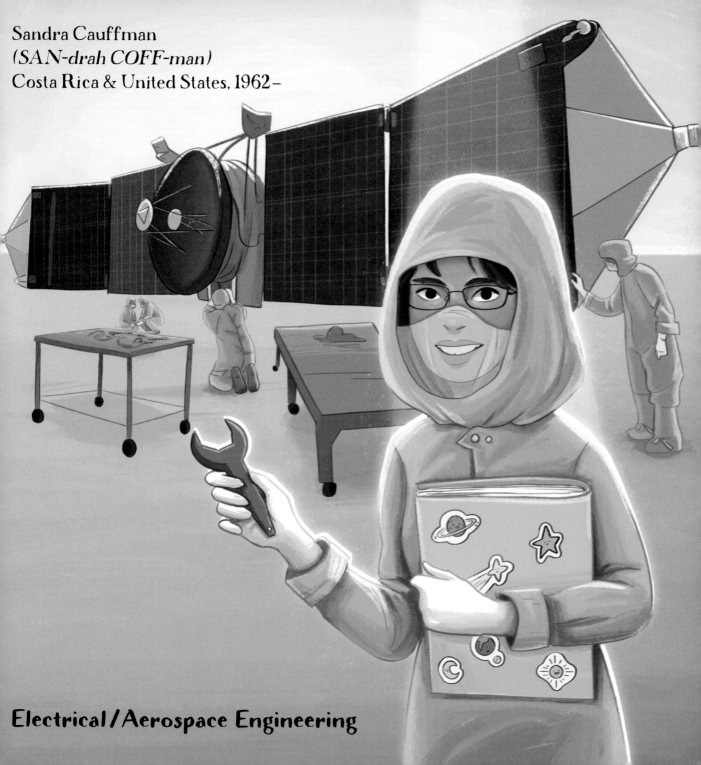

Sandra Cauffman
(SAN-drah COFF-man)
Costa Rica & United States, 1962–

Electrical / Aerospace Engineering

Where do engineers
get their inspiration?

Engineers get inspiration from just about anywhere. Sandra was inspired by watching the moon landing when she was seven years old.

Dr. Treena Livingston Arinzeh was inspired by working in a lab that helped people with injuries. She became a biomedical engineer, or as she says, "An engineer of the body." On her mission to use engineering to help people with illnesses and disabilities, Dr. Treena has made some amazing medical discoveries.

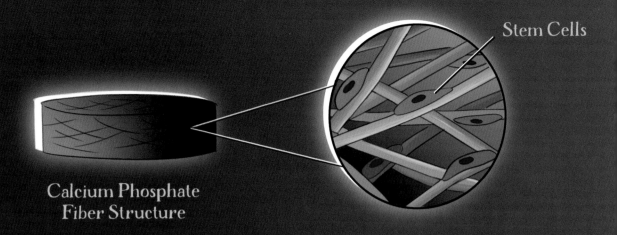

Stem Cells

Calcium Phosphate
Fiber Structure

Hoping to help bones heal, Dr. Treena found a way to transplant adult stem cells—powerful cells that don't have a job yet—into the body. But to heal severe injuries and disabilities, Dr. Treena knew a structure was needed to help the cells grow.

After many experiments in her laboratory, she discovered that she could build a structure for growing bone cells out of a material called calcium phosphate.

Dr. Treena Livingston Arinzeh
(TREE-nah LIV-ing-sten ah-RIN-zeh)
United States, 1970–

Biomedical Engineering

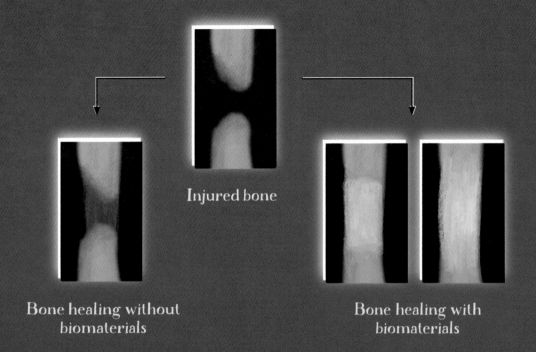

Injured bone

Bone healing without
biomaterials

Bone healing with
biomaterials

These kinds of structures are known as biomaterials, and they're placed in the body to help with healing. Dr. Treena's biomaterials also encourage new cells to grow, improving the way the body heals itself.

Dr. Treena has received many awards for her discoveries. Her work with biomaterials could one day help people paralyzed by spinal cord injuries be able to walk again.

Engineers can do so many different things!
Is there one thing they ALL do?

All engineers use the most powerful tool: imagination. They have an idea and strive to make it happen. When faced with challenges, they problem-solve again and again until they achieve their goals. It's not so different from when you use your imagination to tell a story, draw a picture, or do an experiment. When you think creatively to solve a problem, you are using the skills of an engineer.

Engineers bring
dreams into the world.

They build bridges
from imagination...
to reality!

# Glossary

AERODYNAMIC: Shaped in a way that lets an object fly easily through the air.

AEROSPACE ENGINEER: A person who designs, builds, and works with spacecraft, aircraft, satellites, and missiles.

ALCHEMY: An early version of chemistry based on transforming metals into gold.

BIOMATERIAL: Something placed into the human body to help with healing bone and tissue.

BIOMEDICAL ENGINEER: A person who designs, builds, and works with technology that is made to improve health.

CALCIUM PHOSPHATE: A mineral found in human bones and teeth.

CHEMICAL ENGINEER: A person who designs, builds, and works on equipment and processes involving chemicals.

CHIEF ENGINEER: An engineer who oversees a project by managing workers, coordinating supplies, and giving directions.

CIVIL ENGINEER: A person who designs, builds, and works on projects that are useful to a community, such as bridges, roads, and water systems.

ELECTRICAL ENGINEER: A person who designs, builds, and works with equipment and technology involving electricity.

**ENGINEER:** A person who solves a problem by designing, building, and working on machines, tools, structures, and other technologies.

**EXPERIMENT:** A test to collect information about the world to see if a hypothesis is correct.

**FREQUENCY:** The number of waves (like radio waves or sound waves) that pass by per second.

**HYPOTHESIS:** An educated guess that a person makes to explain something they think is true or will happen.

**MECHANICAL ENGINEER:** A person who designs, builds, and works on all types of machines, including cars and robots.

**PATENT:** A document that makes sure an invention can only be made and sold by the person who invented it for a certain number of years.

**RADIO WAVE:** Energy that travels in a wave shape, used to send and receive messages in the form of electrical signals which are then converted to information, pictures, or sound.

**SATELLITE:** An object that orbits around a larger object, like a planet, and is designed to collect information.

**STEM CELLS:** Cells that can turn into any type of cell in the body.

**SUSPENSION BRIDGE:** A bridge that is held up by cables anchored to large towers.

**TRANSPLANT:** To take something from one place and put it somewhere else.

Science Wide Open: Women in Engineering
Copyright © 2022 Genius Games, LLC
Original series concept by John J. Coveyou

Written by Mary Wissinger
Illustrated by Danielle Pioli

Published by Science, Naturally!
English hardback first edition • September 2022 • ISBN: 978-1-938492-52-5
English paperback first edition • September 2022 • ISBN: 978-1-938492-53-2
English eBook first edition • September 2022 • ISBN: 978-1-938492-54-9

Spanish edition coming March 2023.

Enjoy all the titles in the series:
    Women in Biology • Las mujeres en la biología
    Women in Chemistry • Las mujeres en la química
    Women in Physics • Las mujeres en la física
    Women in Engineering • Las mujeres en la ingeniería
    Women in Medicine • Las mujeres en la medicina
    Women in Botany • Las mujeres en la botánica

Teacher's Guide available at the Educational Resources page of ScienceNaturally.com.

Published in the United States by:
    Science, Naturally!
        An imprint of Platypus Media, LLC
    750 First Street NE, Suite 700 • Washington, D.C. 20002
    202-465-4798 • Fax: 202-558-2132
    Info@ScienceNaturally.com • ScienceNaturally.com

Distributed to the trade by:
    National Book Network (North America)
        301-459-3366 • Toll-free: 800-462-6420
        CustomerCare@NBNbooks.com • NBNbooks.com
    NBN international (worldwide)
        NBNi.Cservs@IngramContent.com • Distribution.NBNi.co.uk

Library of Congress Control Number: 2022937699

10  9  8  7  6  5  4  3  2  1

Printed in the United States of America.